SEA
SALT

Poems of a Decade 2004–2014

David Mason

"Go to the heart of things, therein irony does not reside, Rilke tells us. These words came to my mind often as I read this newest collection from one of our country's finest poets. Mason's formal excellence is cause enough to celebrate these poems, but it is the emotional honesty, sentiment not sentimentality, that makes *Sea Salt* such a deeply moving and memorable reading experience."

—Ron Rash

"David Mason's poems are about moments of realisation. Something is otherwise. Something has been learned with pain and still it won't settle. There are families moving through houses and institutions, ageing, losing grip, and there are the young and rising and memories of youth. The language is humane, unfussy, firm, moving but not calculated to move. And beyond the personal there is the country as it spreads through its inhabitants and leaves its mark on nature. 'Nobody gave me a god,' ends one poem, 'so I perfect my idolatry of doubt.' It is the doubt that is moving, the way it rounds itself and speaks."

—George Szirtes

Sea Salt

Poems of a Decade
2004–2014

David Mason

Red Hen Press | *Pasadena, CA*

Book layout and design by Natasha Castro

Library of Congress Cataloging-in-Publication Data

Mason, David, 1954–
  [Poems. Selections]
  Sea Salt : Poems of a Decade : 2004–2014 / David Mason.—First Edition.
    pages cm
  ISBN 978-1-59709-965-3
  I. Title.
  PS3563.A7879S43 2014
  811'.54—dc23

2013030245

The Los Angeles County Arts Commission, the National Endowment for the Arts, the Pasadena Arts & Cultural Commission and the City of Pasadena Cultural Affairs Division, the Los Angeles Department of Cultural Affairs, the Dwight Stuart Youth Fund, and Sony Pictures Entertainment partially support Red Hen Press.

First Edition
Published by Red Hen Press
www.redhen.org

Acknowledgments

Poems in this book first appeared in the following periodicals: *Angle*, *The Able Muse*, *The Dark Horse*, *Great River Review*, *Harper's*, *The Hudson Review*, *Image*, *Kin*, *Narrative*, *The New Criterion*, *The New Yorker*, *New Walk*, *Ploughshares*, *Poetry*, *Prairie Schooner*, *Radio Silence*, *The Sewanee Review*, *The Threepenny Review*, *The Times Literary Supplement*, *The Virginia Quarterly Review*.

"Mrs. Mason and the Poets" was reprinted in *Best American Poetry 2012*, edited by Mark Doty.

"The Teller" first appeared on the "Poem-a-Day" website published by The Academy of American Poets (Poets.org).

"Fog Horns" was reprinted in *Poetry: A Pocket Anthology*, edited by R. S. Gwynn. It also appeared in *New Poets of the American West*, edited by Lowell Jaeger.

"Home Care" was reprinted in *Beyond Forgetting: Poems and Prose About Alzheimer's Disease*, edited by Holly Hughes.

"4 July 11" was reprinted in the *Alhambra Poetry Calendar, 2013*, edited by Shafiq Naz. Other poems in this book appeared in previous editions of the calendar.

for Chrissy
Mate

Contents

One ◆

Two ◆ ◆

Three ◆ ◆ ◆

Sea Salt

One ◆

Kéfi

Every meal a communion.
The uninvited dead are here.
Do they miss the taste of wine
or the flickering glare

of the candle in the window?
I remember some of their names.
Their appetites are hollow.
They crowd like moths to the flame

but the poor things cannot burn.
Light-headed in this company,
I look at them all in turn.
The Greeks would call this *kéfi*,

ineffable, weightless, tuned
to the conversations of the night
with or without a moon.
O everything's all right.

It's *kéfi*—coffee would wreck it,
or too much wine, but a song
if I can remember it
will carry us along.

New World

Snow in the pines, spring snow, and a white cloud
glowering, smoke blown from that old pacer
who pauses for all day, and then moves on.

The felled trees lie in the steaming forest
lit by the far coals of the world's beginning.
The fox darts over jeweled kinnikinnik—

Be quick, be quick, say the black beads of his eyes,
and with any luck our eyes will follow him
as far as a look can take us, darting through sleep

to a new thought, another chance at waking.

A Thorn in the Paw

Once I was a young dog with a big thorn
in its paw, slowly becoming that very thorn,
not the howl but the thing
howled at, importunate, printing in blood.

Others grew up with chrism, incense, law,
but I was exiled from the start to stare
at lightning hurled from the sky
into a lake that revealed only itself.

Others had pews and prayer-shawls, old fathers
telling them when to kneel and what to say.
I had only my eyes
my tongue my nose my skin and feeble ears.

Dove of descent, fat worm of contention,
bogeyman, Author—I can't get rid of you
merely by hating the world
when people behave at their too-human worst.

Birds high up in their summer baldachin
obey the messages of wind and leaves.
Their airy hosannas
can build a whole day out of worming and song.

I've worked at the thorn, I've stood by the shore
of the marvelous, drop-jawed and jabbering.
Nobody gave me a god
so I perfect my idolatry of doubt.

The Teller

He told me, maybe thirty years ago,
he'd met a rawboned Eskimo named Jack
while filming polar bears on an ice floe.
Jack went out fishing in his sealskin kayak
but the current carried him so far off course
that when a Russian freighter rescued him
they signed him as a mate to Singapore.
Five years at sea it took to get back home.

The year an Englishman gave him his name.
The year of hustling on a Bali beach.
The year of opium in Viet Nam.
The year he pined for snow. The year he searched
for any vessel that would turn toward Nome.
The man who told me? I tell you, I don't know.

The Fawn

The vigil and the vigilance of love . . .

Sitter to three towheaded, rowdy boys,
the spoiled offspring of the local doctor,
our cousin Maren came north for a summer
and brought us stories of the arid south—
cowpokes and stone survivals.

                One afternoon
she summoned two of us to the garage,
a leaning shed with workbench, vise, and tools
stood up between dark studs and logging chains.
A cobwebbed window faced the windy lake
and let in light that squared off on the floor,
and there, quick-breathing on the cracked concrete,
a wounded fawn's black eyes looked back at us.
Maren told how a neighbor's dog had caught it,
showed us the wheezing holes made by the teeth,
the spotted fur blood-flecked, the shitty haunch
where it had soiled itself in the lunged attack.
Don't know where its mama got to, Maren said.
Poor thing's scared. Don't touch it. Run get a bowl
for water.

         When I came back she made a bed
of tarps and grass. Our tomboy cousin had hauled
that wounded fawn down from the neighbor's field.
Now she nursed it until dusk. Our father
stopped by with his satchel after rounds

and Maren held the fawn so he could listen.
Shaking his head, he sat back on his heels,
removed the stethoscope. He called the vet
who told him there was nothing they could do
but wait it out.

        I don't know, our father said.
Sometimes you shouldn't interfere with nature.

A mean dog isn't nature, Maren said.

Well I'm not blaming you for being kind.

Our father brought a blanket from the house,
a baby bottle filled with milk, and he
and Maren shared the vigil for the fawn,
leaving a light on as they might for a child
sick in some farmer's house.

        Three days—a week—
and father backed the car to the garage
to carry out the dead fawn in a tarp
and bury it in some deep part of the woods,
unmarked, and later unremarked upon
with summer over and our cousin gone.

◆ ◆

If I tell you it was 1963
you'll know a world of change befell us next,

but maybe it was '62. I know
it was before the war divided us
and more than that, before our parents grew
apart like two completely different species,
desert and woods, cactus and thorny vine,
before our nation had its family quarrel,
never quite emerging from it. We boys
had sprouted into trouble of all kinds,
three would-be rebels from a broken home,
and when I next saw Maren, a rancher's wife
in Colorado, she was all for Jesus,
getting saved and saving every day
in some denomination she invented.
We gave up calling and we never write.

The vigil and the vigilance. Our troubles
happened, but were smaller than a country's.
My older brother died at twenty-eight—
an accident in mountains. Our mother sobered
up two decades later. Father died
so far removed from his former sanity
I struggle to remember who he was.

The years are a great winnowing of lives,
but we had knelt together by the fawn
and felt the silence intervene like weather.
I'm still there, looking at that dying fawn,
at how a girl's devotion almost saved it,
wet panic in its eyes, its shivering breath,
its wild heart beating on the concrete floor.

Lieutenant Mason

You have to stuff it all back in,
the gut from a nicked
peritoneum.

That's what the surgeon's skill
was born to do.
To put it all back in
and close the wound.

When the shell hit amidships
none of your aspirations
mattered any more—

pried steel and oily fire,
boys who called each other men
screaming, their obscene
protrusions,

and that was blood running
from your ears, and yes,
among the parts
awash in spume

over the teak deck,
a penis like a jellyfish,
and the scuppers
gushed blood,

you'd never seen so much of it,
and there was nothing, nothing
you or anyone could do
to put it back.

But you have to put it back.
You have to put it back,
and try hard not to talk

for fear of what will spill.
You have to make each knot
meticulously right.

That's how a lifetime passes,
closing, re-closing the wound,
a million stiches tied in time
denying and re-denying

until you learn to let
it lie and let
it weep,
and open.

Energy

for Dewey Huston

Tell me again about the butterflies,
old friend of my father, bringer of tales,
the gully, mossy rocks of the streambed,
a cool breeze off the glacier high above,
and suddenly butterflies everywhere
as if the air you breathed were blossoming.

I've seen so many things, you said. *I wish
I could write them down.* And when my brother died
you were the alpinist and engineer
who had an explanation where he'd gone,
waving a hand in air. *It's energy,*
you said. *That energy must still be somewhere.*

Ah, but the real life is never written down,
and who could understand the butterflies—
that there were so many, so surprisingly?
Tell me again, old friend, and I will try
to catch the light, the flavor of the air
like moss, like distant ice, like clear water.

Fathers and Sons

Some things, they say,
one should not write about. I tried
to help my father comprehend
the toilet, how one needs
to undo one's belt, to slide
one's trousers down and sit,
but he stubbornly stood
and would not bend his knees.
I tried again
to bend him toward the seat,

and then I laughed
at the absurdity. Fathers and sons.
How he had wiped my bottom
half a century ago, and how
I would repay the favor
if he would only sit.

            Don't you—
he gripped me, trembling, searching for my eyes.
Don't you—but the word
was lost to him. Somewhere
a man of dignity would not be laughed at.
He could not see
it was the crazy dance
that made me laugh,
trying to make him sit
when he wanted to stand.

Home Care

My father says his feet will soon be trees
and he is right, though not in any way
I want to know. A regal woman sees
me in the hallway and has much to say,
as if we were lovers once and I've come back
to offer her a rose. But I am here
to find the old man's shoes, his little sack
of laundered shirts, stretch pants and underwear.

Rattling a metal walker for emphasis,
his pal called Joe has one coherent line—
How the hell they get this power over us?—
then logic shatters and a silent whine
crosses his face. My father's spotted hands
flutter like dying moths. I take them up
and lead him in a paranoiac dance
toward the parking lot and our escape.

He is my boy, regressed at eighty-two
to mooncalf prominence, drugged and adrift.
And I can only play, remembering who
he was not long ago, a son bereft.
Strapped in the car, he sleeps away the hour
we're caught in currents of the interstate.
He will be ashes in a summer shower
and sink to roots beneath the winter's weight.

Mrs. Vitt

The first to realize what a liar I was,
a boy pretending to have read a book
in second grade about a big black cat
(I'd made it as far as the cover silhouette),
the first to let us choose our spelling words
like *telephone* and *information*, long
pronounceable portions of the sky outside,
words I ever after spelled correctly,
the first to tell me I was a funny boy
or had a funny sense of the truth, or had
no sense of it but was funny anyway,
Mrs. Vitt began to shake one day,
lighting her cigarette in the teacher's lounge,
or carrying coffee in her quaking hands.
I was in high school then, but heard she'd quit
and went to visit her in the old north end
of town, and met her thin, attentive husband
strapping her to a board to hold her straight.
She smiled at me, though her head shook to and fro.
It took her husband many lighter flicks
to catch her swaying cigarette. She looked
like a knife-thrower's trembling model. *Mrs. Vitt,*
I blurted out. *I'm sorry.* She stared at me,
but whether she was nodding or shaking *no*
I couldn't tell. *Sorry I lied so much.*
I must have given you a lot of grief.
And she, with each word shuddered out in smoke:
No child I taught was any grief to me.

Driving With Marli

Grandpa, do you live in the sky?
No, but I live on a mountain
and came on a plane to see you.
Why?
All leaping thought and ruminant pool,
a three-year-old is a verbal fountain,
water clear enough to see through.
Anything can fool
the wizard in the front seat of the car.
How far will we go, Grandpa? How far?

Little one, I must re-learn
all subjects such as distances,
study the foolishness and burn
like candlelight to worry less and less
about the night.
It's not that youth is always right
but that an aging man
is too preoccupied with plans.
I do live in the sky,
but I do not know why.

Two ◆ ◆

Waters, plants and stones know this,
That they love, not what love is.
—Thomas Stanley, *"The Magnet"*

Call the world if you please 'The vale
of Soul-making.' Then you will
find out the use of the world . . .
—John Keats, *Letters*

Child

Does it make you sad to see the close
    of the family romance,
to know the house is grounded in the flow
    and left to chance
by currents you never had control of?

    Well, I could say
I'm sorry till the last of all our days.
    My flesh is feeling clay
eroded by more tides than I can blame
    or bring myself to name.

The Nape

In the cidery light of morning
I saw her at the table
reading the paper, her cup
of coffee near at hand,
and that was when I bent
and brushed the hair from her nape
and kissed the skin there, breathing
the still surprising smoothness
of her skin against my lips—
stolen, she might say,
as if I would be filled
with joy of touching her,
I the fool for love,
and all that history carried
back to me in the glide
of mouth on skin, knowledge
of who she is by day
and night, sleeping lightly,
rocked in gentle privacy,
or outside in the garden
probing earth and planting.
We had been this way for more
than twenty years, she
leading a life of purpose
rarely stated, and I
just back from somewhere else.
I brushed my lips on her skin
and felt her presence through me,
her elegant containment
there in the cidery light.

The Future

The future, best greeted
without luggage in hand,
outside the terminal
where trees behave as they will,
dressing, undressing,
or dressed to kill,

where we are the species
birthing ideas
from our eyes from our hands
our ears our skin,
from soil in our pores
and love we pour out

in letters and emails—
the future is always
more open than we think,
though not for some,
the warnings remind us,
not for some.

Like you I am trying
to leave my luggage
behind in the car
or the circling carousel, walk
open handed
from terminal doors.

Because like you
I have walked and flown

through calendar hours,
dreamed through minutes and years
and the breadcrumb days
I leave by the road . . .

We know we are nothing,
forgetting our names
or the names of the cities,
the nothing we know as we know
the light on a window,
river of rivers.

The Wards

No story could explain them,

the murdering eyes
through meshed plexiglass windows,

their wailing
and their shit-smeared cells,

the nightmare pacers,
the near and dear I hold at bay—

their staining shame
and medicated stares.

They come back singing
an exhausted song

of what was done to them,
how money cannot ward off everything.

I see them now in the park,
as much at a loss in daylight
as at home in the dark.

They drag their living to the stream
that runs behind the buildings
in a secret dream.

They nurse their lurid sores
and suck from paper bags.

They are drawn to water,
to emerging leaves
above the litter of bottle glass.

Some days I breathe like a man
in an iron lung, a puff-fish

in a soiled canal,
remembering the frightened
letters of the mad.

I sent those letters from another life.

Some days I pray
they won't betray me to the wards.

The Man Who Lied

All his life he was touch and run,
word man turned by an inner eel
that shocked him hourly till he was numb.
What is a heart but something to steal?

Scab man, scar man, scolding himself,
making love but a troubled lover,
forgetting his soul on a kitchen shelf
to seek it daily, yearly, forever.

Giver, talker, crazy friend,
why all the running? When will it end?

Out

When thunder tore the dark
I woke and smelled the rain
alone in another house
and all that held me gone.

I'd hurt you in the night
and left the day to bleed
and cast my self away
to chance it like a weed.

In the Barber Shop

The woman barber clips and combs and clips
a woman's hair, always solicitous,
touching her customer with utmost care,
while at the footrest a loving husband kneels,
consoling his frail wife in Polish, holding
her trembling hands in his big, clement hands.

Why is the wife (so thin and aged) afraid?
Why is the barber holding back her tears?
A stroke maybe? Maybe long history
related in those calming, murmured words.
And even if you've seen such love before
there's shame in having left it at the door,

in having thought too often of oneself
and present happiness. The husband pays
and wheels his whimpering, child-like wife outside
where winter sunlight strikes the anvil street,
and helicopter blades of light leap out
from windshields in the supermarket lot.

Now try to meet the barber's eyes, and take
your seat and let her pin the collar on.
Her touch, all business, has a healing power
but not enough, or not enough for you.
And when you pay and leave and feel the cold,
the dicing blades of light will scatter you.

Sarong Song

The woman in the blue sarong
bade me believe in ships.
Come sail with me, the journey's long,
sang her alluring lips

that baited me in a net of words
and hauled me to her bed
at the top of the world where thieving birds
loved me till I bled.

I came from an underworld of snow,
she from a windy dune.
She dared to look for me below
the phases of the moon.

Come walk with me, the journey's joy,
she sang with her blue eyes.
Untie the sarong, my bonny boy,
and bare me to the skies.

Necessity

Below the blinkered traffic on the road,
almost unseen, the creek falls as it must,
called by downhill, called by the waxing moon—
who judges how its clarity responds?

As night pours in, I hunker on the bank
below a water birch, and watch the light
contend with not-light in the pools and channels,
the way a boulder or a gravel bar

can bend the current without altering
necessity, the bed-ward conversation.
The water talks like an old woman known
for knowing names of every man she touched.

She goes on falling, falling, you might say,
unfailingly, the one consistent joy
from snowmelt on the peak to this plain dirt,
pebbles and kayak leaves marooned on twigs,

while I am crouching in the dark, betrayed
by distances. I think again of you
who love the water and are far away,
and I go falling where the water goes.

The Tarmac

Lack, you say? The world will strip you naked.
Time you realized it. Too many years
you worked in a plush denial, head down,
dodging yourself as much as others.

Nobody did this to you.
Trained in deafness, you soon went blind,
but gathered strength for metamorphosis
in order to become your kind.

Now nothing helps but silence as you learn
slowly the letting go,
and learn again, and over again, again,
blow upon blow,

you must go by the way of mountain tides,
coral blizzards and the sunlit rain.
The wave of nausea heaves
and passes through the egocentric pain

and finds you on a tarmac going where
your skin and hair, eyes, ears and fingers feel
a change is in the air.
You are unfolding now, and almost real.

Another Thing

Like fossil shells embedded in a stone,
you are an absence, rimmed calligraphy,
a mouthing out of silence, a way to see
beyond the bedroom where you lie alone.
So why not be the vast, antipodal cloud
you soloed under, riven by cold gales?
And why not be the song of diving whales,
why not the plosive surf below the road?

The others are one thing. They know they are.
One compass needle. They have found their way
and navigate by perfect cynosure.
Go wreck yourself once more against the day
and wash up like a bottle on the shore,
lucidity and salt in all you say.

Prayer to the Air

Teach me to breathe, that I know I am not drowning.
Teach me to break like the lightning-scalded tree.
Teach me to love that love is never owning.
Teach me. Teach me.

I am the stain of blood spilled on the glacial snow.
I am the ashes washed by rain from the scree.
I am the trembling man who kneels for hours below.
Teach me. Teach me.

I have taken the knife coldly to some I love.
I have killed beauty, allowing beauty to be
before the fear could kill me. Storms above,
teach me. Teach me.

Let It Go

Earth, I walked on a trail of blooming dryad,
lay on a boulder, watching night come on,
the eager silhouetted limbs thrust up,
harmless night known first in a darker blue
then even darker to the dust of stars,
the far off traffic of a night-denying city,
the dogs calling, I thought, joyfully. Night,
harmless night when my love moves in her day
on the far side of Earth, an ocean away.

Today a friend called, his voice thick with grief
because he cannot stop himself from feeling,
because his joy and grief are the same chord
on the same bowed *lyra*. My friend is Greek, the *lyra*
no mere symbol but a mode of living, fire
in the night, cold water at dawn. And you, Earth,
have called out to us all our lives, in squall
and zephyr, flood and tidal wave, no one life
enough to hear the chord beyond belief.

Earth, I am learning mineral patience, moved
by the current of last night's dreaming, this morning's coffee.
Sometimes I hate you for coming between my love
and me, for being so large, so full of laws
and nations and money and people who cling to them all.
I know it is not your wish. I try to live
with animal resignation, grazing the weather,
alert for signs of danger. We've just begun,
my love and I, to meet beneath the sun.

We live each day in the shade of another life,
anonymous as all of space, or all
that passes under the canopy of leaves.
Earth, we cannot cling to you any more
than to each other. The life already over
is the one we love, the tears already shed,
the words already written, the magic drowned,
our feeling fire that sparks into the stars
while down below the ordinary cars

go on, abrasive and efficient commerce,
the houses glow and people lock their doors.
I'm shedding what I own, or trying to,
walking down the path of blooming dryad
and the pitch of pines, until I hear the stream
below me in the canyon, below the road,
below the traffic of ambition and denial,
the unclear water running to the sea,
the stream, dear Earth, between my love and me.

4 July 11

From over the ridge, chrysanthemums of fire
burst into color. One hears the pop-pop-pop
of another birthday, but the heart is flat champagne.

Who cares about freedom, and *Damn King George*?
Who cares about sirens out in city lights?
I've got enough to fight about right here,

the howitzer let loose inside my ribs,
the thudding ricochet from hill to hill,
from hurt to hurt. Hard birth. Hard coming to.

When I Didn't Get the News

I was on the Welsh coast, off
St. David's, on a bluff
looking down on the Atlantic

with Chrissy (chicken sandwiches,
strawberries and champagne
might have been the thing).

Instead, we drove
to the Snowdonian sunset
and returned to the full,
the rising moon.

◆ ◆

I didn't get the news,
but slowly through the night
slept out the sweat of ages
channeled like a current over stones,

and woke to a day as calm and ordinary
as a blur of hedgerow,
a sunlit quarter of portioned field.

Small roadside phalanxes of foxglove
marshaled me to peace.

And that was when,
long after it had happened,
I did get the news,
or my computer did,

the simple fact that you were dead
and that I'd missed the whole final drama
while in my life.

◆ ◆ ◆

The day of sunlight on the swales
and lowing cattle, glowing coals
of hillside sheep,

the day of fantasies about the perfect hovel
on the hill, the day we would try
to keep,

that day was the day my mother died,
simple fact—a useful thing, that—
and became *not here*

across thousands of miles of sea
and air.

◆ ◆ ◆ ◆

I tried to think of who you were,
and how you tried to tell me at the end
to let go the whole baggage of the past.

No sense in grinding it to sausage,
no sense in cooking it to the perfect
killing meal.

The particular you, the wry jokes
and walking stick, the book groups
and bad girls who loved you—

might as well let them in
as they were the ones who knew you best,
the beautiful blind and halt,

the whisky-soaked and all the rest
forgiven as they had forgiven you.

And I am with them too.

14 July 11

Where does a life go? Can't
answer that, can't go
where the holy rollers go.

I like the clouds, though,
above the hills at Brecon.
As trees are clouds,

as blown roses
and my love too, all cloud,
all rain, I reckon.

Salmon Leap

The only constant was the sound of water,
and we, gill-breathing moss
and learning love would be there when we sought her,
prepared ourselves for loss.

Wherever absences are crossed by day
without a touch or look,
whenever there is nothing we can say,
remember the talking brook.

There is no deeper sleep than in the stream,
however it may fall
or heave in tides upon a distant dream.
Whatever voices call,

our ashes will be washed away by rain
and we will speak aloud
the language of a watery refrain,
clear as any cloud.

Night and My Love

Old darkness gathers in the leaves
before it enters breath, before the whole of night
comes rushing on a current down to take her
where it will, and she fulfills her obligation to the dusk
only by surrendering to all it is and renders.

Night, sweet night beyond the lamps
and desperate moths like men that can't let go of her,
short night in summer, the blink of an eye up north,
where stars can barely show themselves before
dawn snuffs them like faint coals of a fire,

come sweet oblivion, repair
the harm another day abraded on us, my love
in pain I can do nothing to assuage.
Come morphine pills, come valium
and give her the small assurances you offer.

She only wants to sleep a while
and try to walk again, the nerves
massaged by arms of the least demanding god,
the genius of erasure, and the voice
of water pending evermore.

Come night. I love you for the way
each day surrenders to you wholly,
for the moon that bleeds through boughs above the stream.
Come stream of darkness, moths, migrations
mitigating all excess of planning.

Come tell us stories from the stars,
come suffocate us with your love,
come break the precious household,
break the bed in furious loving,
break all of us upon your bluest anvil.

Night, I beg you, night,
anoint me with anonymity,
annul my neediness, my expectations,
and let my love sleep on and wake
annealed, anew, and ever after

wholly in herself and in her day,
and know my gratitude is simple.
Know I am alive to who I am.
Know me, night, your humble servant,
lover, here and now, of all you tender.

"All Change"

A call in a flickering tunnel
packed with human multiforms.

Dash up the down escalator
gasping like a salmon,

but not so solemnly,
onto the rain-wet pavement.

All change, all change, born
to spawn and die,

the river maiden plunges hands
in the lukewarm Thames,

the brown eddy and flow,
and calls it blessed.

You've seen her swim
in total delight

and weather change.
Water's her nature

and water's life,
there for the drinking.

The Quire

She stands at the effigy of Donne
and tears erupt
from lines a lifetime gone.

His combed beard and heightened cheeks,
eyes closed in the lightest sleep,
lips that sermoned pursed in secret peace,

robed knees that will no longer kneel,
almost a lion wan with piety,
he resembles someone known

through sun and rain. There she
remains—my true love crying
at a man again.

Lop-Sided Prayer

Bluejoint, fescue, foxglove, bee-sipped daisies
sign to the breeze what its direction is.

The night bleeds into everything you see.
Oh please be you. And please let me be me.

Mind

The kayak passes in a glide—not birds,
but children chattering along the shore.

The decades come in waves, the waves pass on
and echo back from rocks below the firs,

a sound already gone. You've seen the dead
become their sifted ashes while the lake

changes and does not change hue. Ever since
the ice withdrew. Until the ice comes back.

The Dying Man

After a week a man in a brown suit
appeared at the foot of the bed. They talked
a language of sunlight inside window glass
while family eyed each other wonderingly.

I also stood by the bed and held his hand
and brushed his hair and touched his beard.
He smiled and said, *No tears, but it's good to see
old friends.* In the kitchen women unwrapped food,

and in the garden everything was good.

Our Dead

Now let them fold their hands and try no more
the nets and reels. Let them sit
athwart the gunwales of an open boat
and say they have no need of a catch tonight.

It is enough to see gillnetters' lights
glow brighter as the daylight's bleeding out,
enough to hear the suck
and plash of waves against a tossing hull,

as boat and brine are the sleepiest of lovers,
mere surfaces that know
how many moving depths there are
above the deck and below the sole.

The calmest night we ever watched at sea—
make that the night they wonder in.
No one expects them home.
The moon will not forbid their wandering.

Nor are they really ours, of course.
We only navigate that way,
by something named, some story told
to last until the day.

Presently

A small girl sobbing in the beached canoe—
oh *never, never* will she be consoled.
And while across the lawn and deep in shade
her sister shuts the tree house in a sulk,
another girl goes flying on a rope
beneath the aged cedar's drooping limbs.

All true, all going on, still going on
as the quiet uncle watches from the lawn
where he stands arm in arm with someone dead.
He sees the cautious foraging of doe
and fawn along the lakeside fringe of alders—
all presently occurring. The forming waves

reform, the windblown hair of children waves
and voices call, and someday tears will dry.
It is a day for walking heedfully,
a day for looking up and looking out
where some go flying and where others fall
and find the consolation of the dead.

The Insert

Change planes, change lives,
and why should any memory intervene?

The bridge you crossed
from school the day before you turned fourteen,

and found, behind
Bart's Mobil Station, two Lummi Indian girls

locked in a fight,
both grunting. One yanked the other's ironed curls

and tried to hold
her blouse together over heavy breasts.

Screaming now,
the other bled from nose and mouth, thickening gouts

that smeared her face
and stained the first girl's hands. You felt the hurt

and parted them
and stanched the bleeding with your balled-up shirt,

then walked away,
chilled in t-shirt, shouldering your bag of books.

And never saw
those girls again, except in sideways looks.

Change lives, change planes,
change anything you walk to or away from.

None of it stays
in place. None of it knows a trace of reason.

Die When You Die

You, friend, have far to go. You cannot change
another and you cannot change yourself.
Let be. Weep when it is time for weeping,
laugh when laughter comes. No one else alive
will have a say in that.

Die when you die.

Night Song

The breeze around our bed
cooling the summer night
is looking, looking for you,
except it has no sight,

so it must feel my skin
and probe the sheet for yours
and wonder where you've gone,
and wander on its course.

I keep the door ajar
to let the blindness in,
and dream in its embrace
of you, your touch, your skin.

The Laudromat in Sunlight

These our hymns
to changing, heads
of launderers bent
over their readings, faces
turned to think of remarking
What a marvel it is
to soften fabric, to make
a warm skin next
to the skin you live in—
a passing intercourse the sun
dissolves, solution of time
for the great unwashed,
the wishful tuned to the hum
of the tumbling dryers.

Come, join our number.
You need not speak a word.

One Another

What current between us
touches abandoned days
to the present of yes?

Your face on the pillow
rapt in a distant glow
of self-loss, undertow,

drawn out deeper than love—
how will the days evolve,
the evenings believe

that what we are, we may
be without asking why,
given without a way.

As you are. That's how I
would have you be
if I had any say.

River Days

These are the hours, those the willow stems,
aspen and cottonwood giving away their gold.
Such is our stillness, watching the same wave
where only the water changes.
What was it we differed over?

◆

Day and night the river roars—or does it hush?
A noise akin to wordlessness
but for the syllables of crow and hawk,
the clack of shifting rocks.
And we? We are beside ourselves at last.

◆

You stared into the canyoned years,
millions of them, where the water-saw
lowered the river bed so far
that we could only gape, our minds leaping.
We must mean what we say,

the way the gorge reveals its earliest foldings,
the way it waits for us to learn the ground
we walk upon, cousin to the cold
and distant planets, the way it watches us
by being seen and partly understood.

◆

That there should be this
abundance even in a desert, the wild
buckwheat, snowberry, mountain mahogany,
that gneiss and pegamite should color cliffs
cut by the green river laughing below,

is cause enough for praise,
but that you should join me here
and joyfully hold my hand, that I should forget
the wristwatch in my pocket as I pace the day
is love beyond measure.

◆

Like others of our kind we move toward water,
not only to slake our thirst
but also because it binds us,
our tides and metamorphoses, our bed
of scars, our love, our passing.

From a Side Yard

The truck, a relic
rusting in the shade,
drove from another
century to this
punctured standstill,
a weird flute in the wind.

With its cracked glass
and metal and warped
boards it admits you
to the far
gallery of grass,
the hills brushed

by rivering death,
that other road
beside the road you travel,
an artery still
running under ice,
a loyalty, a life.

Leavings

How naked, how bereft
that wall of picture hooks
where faces used to make me cringe,
how bare the shelves
unloaded of their library, how like
another life the furnace
sighs to an empty house,
the decades it took a dresser
to leave its carpet mark,
its unvacuumed blur of dust.

Of six who lived here once
four are dead.
They've gone out before us.
I close the door, haunted.

The Oregon Way

Gone are the curls of smoke,
gone are the tears in the eyes.
They've vanished up the coughing flue
into the pouring skies.

It's rain that holds us in
and makes us look without—
the sateen mosses on the trees,
hornwort, liverwort.

Wring out the clouds, my lady.
Tumble them into your arms.
We're passing all day the wet bales of hay
on soft fermenting farms

where sloughs and marshes darken,
salted by rising tides,
and the wet squalls charge at the wipers,
and only the road abides.

At the Sylvia Beach Hotel

It may be the perfect surf,
its heavenly OM,
or the library shelves, the warm
tea on the side table,
the rain-tapped window
where gulls glide on their sails
that makes you exclaim
I could live here forever!

It may be the wish
to be washed in the sea air
daily till your pages fill
and your lettered life
has flooded and over-spilled.

In the sailor's home of the mind
let the soluble hours
declare themselves and pass.
Let the softened spines
of a whole row of books
remind you how far,
how familiar are your travels.

The Seaside Distances

Each solitary figure could be driftwood
until it moves, becoming man and dog,
brothers playing tag or a girl with a kite.

On a beached log a tumult of crabbing gulls,
and beyond that brawl each curled pursuing wave
dies on the wave that died ahead of it,
as something in me died when you walked out
to nurse a hurt in that inhuman space.

Nothing worked for either but the sea
where I interrogated every shape
that was not you, and nothing answered me.

Only the sea dissolving us could help,
the knots of kelp and carcasses of birds,
the patterned sand and hummocks of salt grass,
and when we found each other in the room
our drowning made it possible to grieve.

A Deafness

For days now at the mouth of the stream,
at the gray seam of gravel and sky,
a bald eagle has watched from pilings
kokanee moving inland to spawn.

The landlocked salmon dart past shallows
where he can feed, a lord at leisure.
They fan in alder-shadowed pools
until they die without a fight.

For we who cannot hear, this happens
with a more impartial love,
unruffled motion, like wet leaves
already fallen. No regret,

no whining need, no infant hurt,
nothing to say we're sorry for,
no chance to try again. A sinking,
used and belly-up in the stream.

And we keep going back to listen
through the moving shadows, the glide
and turn of bodies we have known,
to the deep evaders of desire.

She Is

a small wolf eating a caul

a girl holding the leg
of a broken doll

a true egg
fertilized by a swan

warm gold in the water
but a cold dawn

after the slaughter

a hurt tune
lying still in a dark room

a knapsack crammed with words
unpacked

repacked
like a deck of cards

a sine curve
in a line of thought

all nerve
uncaught

Chrismata

How could they know,
how could anyone know
you were not formed by origins,

a family colder than a well
of fears? No ordinary rule applies
because you've died already,
died and died,

as fresh annointings—salt, baptismal rain—
become the ritual made new
by moving on and moving through.

The Soul Fox

for Chrissy, 28 October 2011

My love, the fox is in the yard.
The snow will bear his print a while,
then melt and go, but we who saw
his way of finding out, his night
of seeking, know what we have seen
and are the better for it. Write.
Let the white page bear the mark,
then melt with joy upon the dark.

Three ◆ ◆ ◆

Amaknak

After a shift of killing crab by thousands
you punch out in the dark companionway
and walk the plank from hull to gravel quay
to make good use of the last rain of the day
for squinting into, booting it by the sea.
The lives you held in your hands

were split in two, but were they really mute
when legs and claws went into the boiling bins,
when brain and back were ground to a fine powder?
You walk the thought off, leaning into the wind
as onto the rocks the surf pounds harder and harder.
Death is never remote.

It follows you like a brother in ptarmigan hills.
Death in the ruined bunker of somebody's war
where shattered glass and condoms strew the floor,
the whistling wind and tapping strand of wire.
Death in the drunken fisherman's stony stare
and the storm of mewling gulls.

Death in the open stench of a rotting seal.
Death in the bleached tangle of driftwood limbs.
Death in the sunken fleet in Captain's Bay
and the bay itself where schools of sockeye swim.
Death in the weather having its rainy way,
the way you learn to fail.

For sooner or later the shore will turn you around.
You follow its edge to the steaming barge where you work,
rain in the work-lights, beams in a driven cloud,
death in the daylight, death in the coming dark,
death in the song you forgetfuly sing aloud
over the shell-covered ground.

Incantation

All confounded marriages, all ideals
conforming out of lethargy or lies,
hopes flattened or impaled, untimely deaths,
delusions, prisons and escapes, all wars
crawling on bloody hands to no conclusion,
all speeches, protest signs and poetry,
all schools and rules and eagerness to please,
priestly demarcations of the one law,
all chrome desired, all vintage poured, possessions
bought, sold, bartered, had and lost
are nothing to the auricles and sheaths,
spikelets and seedheads of an ordinary
end-of-summer clump of roadside grass,
green-violet and fawn and gold and brown,
bird-jointed, wind-steady, unseen, and seen.

Praying with a Friend

That gecko panting on the whitewashed wall,
only witness in the little chapel
where I pay my coin and light a beeswax candle—
deference applied unasked for. Given.

Whatever gods have lived at Kalamitsi,
I know, as many locals do, the spring
now hidden by a thorny cloud of brambles.
It fed my garden once. I drank from it

the clearest water I have ever known,
medium of shade and other voices.

Mrs. Mason and the Poets

At that point I had lived with Mr. Tighe
so many years apart from matrimony
we quite forgot the world would call it sin.
We were, in letters of our friends at Pisa,
Mr. and Mrs. Mason, the common name
domesticating the arrangement. (Our friends
were younger, thinking it a novelty.)

You've heard about Lord Byron and his zoo,
how he befriended geese he meant to eat
and how they ruled his villa like a byre
with peacocks, horses, monkeys, cats and crows.
And our friend Shelley whom we thought so ill,
whose brilliant wife was palely loitering,
waiting to give birth and dreading signs
that some disaster surely must befall them.
Shelley of the godless vegetable love,
pursuer of expensive causes, sprite.
He had confided in me more than once
how his enthusiasms caused him pain
and caused no end of pain to those he loved.

Some nights I see his blue eyes thrashing back
and comprehend how grieved he was, how aged.
Genius, yes, but often idiotic.
It took too many deaths, too many drownings,

fevers, accusations, to make him see
the ordinary life was not all bad.

I saw him last, not at the stormy pier
but in a dream. He came by candlelight,
one hand inside a pocket, and I said,
You look ill, you are tired, sit down and eat.

He answered, *No, I shall never eat more.
I have not a* soldo *left in all the world.*

Nonsense, this is no inn—you need not pay.

Perhaps it is the worse for that, he said.
He drew the hand out of his pocket, holding
a book of poems as if to buy his supper.
To see such brightness fallen broke my heart,
and then, of course, I learned that he had drowned.

Once, they say, he spread a paper out
upon a table, dipped his quill and made
a single dot of ink. *That,* he said,
*is all of human knowledge, and the white
is all experience we dream of touching.
If I should spread more paper here, if all
the paper made by man were lying here,
that whiteness would be like experience,
but still our knowledge would be that one dot.*

I've watched so many of the young die young.
As evening falls, I know that Mr. Tighe
will come back from his stroll, and he will say
to humour me, *Why Mrs. Mason, how
might you have spent these several lovely hours?*

And I shall notice how a slight peach flush
illuminates his whiskers as the sun
rounds the palms and enters at our windows.
And I shall say, *As you have, Mr. Mason,
thinking of lost friends, wishing they were here.*

And he: *Lost friends? Then I should pour the wine.*

And I? What shall I say to this kind man
but *Yes, my darling, time to pour the wine.*

Marco Polo in the Old Hotel

Marco . . .

        . . . Polo

Marco . . .

        . . . Polo

Pour another glass of sunlight,
tasting an after-dinner hour.
This is not a time for reading.
Wait a while. A meteor shower
may fall about your head tonight
and children in a nearby pool
are laughing in late summer air,
happy to be free of school.

Marco . . .

        . . . Polo

Marco . . .

        . . . Polo

You are the only dinner guest.
The meal is finished, but the wine
will last until the dark arrives.
The children in the pool incline
their bodies, leaping from the waves,
their voices calling to each other,

traveling through the evenings, years
and decades of late summer weather.

Marco . . .
                    . . . Polo

Marco . . .
                    . . . Polo

Across the parking lot a flag
is flapping, thin as Chinese silk
the camels caravanned through deserts.
Voices fall into the dark.
You breathe the last mouthful of wine
and seem to float into the air
as they call to eternity,
the unenclosing everywhere:

Marco . . .
                    . . . Polo

Marco . . .
                    . . . Polo

Andrítsena Revisited

To sleep among ruins, tall shadows cast
by moonlight across the stone floor, columns
and pediments devoted to the god
long since departed with his relevance,
then hear the special pleading of the place,
again the nightingale deep in the woods—
but that was long ago, before the tent
was raised, shielding the temple from acid rain.

Remember? You woke hungover on the stones
to find a curious fox sat watching you,
the empty bottles where your friends had left them,
the friends themselves, who at their stirring sent
that lithe fox darting among terraced flowers.
The hill is known for foxes even now.

◆

Losing the path, you find Andrítsena
below a maze of red dirt roads, goat folds,
gullies choked with laurel, hawthorn, balm,
thick-waisted oaks with skirts of emerald nettles,
couchgrass, chamomile—and so one world
turns its gaze away and leaves another
privately fruitful, moving at turtle speed
toward what cannot be a destination,

only the slow discovery of noon
when, footsore, you follow the cooking smoke
from hunks of spitted lamb into the village.
Birdsong and barking dogs attend you here,
the spell of secret woods abating, the street
preoccupied with other peoples' lives.

A Sort of Oracle

Late one afternoon between sun and rain
I found the path ascending above Delphi
toward a spring an old man said I would find,
not knowing whom to ask about my life,
the wrongs I may have done myself or others,
and when I'd climbed beyond the yapping dogs
and the last engines of commercial traffic,
I asked an almond tree, an oracle
as good as any, for some forgiving word.

One does these things when nothing else makes sense,
feeling a giddy madness. The tree said nothing,
the cloudy shafts of sunlight stabbed, withdrew,
the cuckoo called from olives down below
its two comedic notes. I found the spring
and drank from it and washed the sweat from my face,
then turned back to the town where friends were waiting.

The Bay of Writing

And I with only a reed in my hands.
—George Seferis

The reed, dried and cut, could make a pan-pipe
on an idle day. I say the word again,
kalamus, that early pen, from breezy
leaf to leaves of nervy writing—Sappho,
Archilochos, their fingering lines,
a silent music till our voices find it.

In retrospect I walk among those trees,
polled mulberries no longer home to silkworms,
the crone-like olives, upright cypresses
above the hammered metal of the bay
called *Kalamitsi*. There the lazy hours
watching the ant roads through the summer straw

taught me the frantic diligence of mind,
the way it ferries breadcrumbs and small seeds
fast fast to its storehouse in reedy shade.
The way the hand rests on an open book
I've disappeared into, takes up a pen
and traces letters in a trail of words.

Kalamus, Kalamitsi, bay of reeds,
music of everything I have not written.

Fog Horns

The loneliest days,
damp and indistinct,
sea and land a haze.

And purple fog horns
blossomed over tides—
bruises being born

in silence, so slow,
so out there, around,
above and below.

In such hurts of sound
the known world became
neither flat nor round.

The steaming tea pot
was all we fathomed
of *is* and *is not*.

The hours were hallways
with doors at the ends
opened into days

fading into night
and the scattering
particles of light.

Nothing was done then.
Nothing was ever
done. Then it was done.

Tree Light House

That slow familiar breathing
is the sea, I remember now,
and rain in the green limbs.
I dreamed your body
warm in the doona,
your unquestioning hands,
and woke to find you
fevered but alive
to be grateful for.

◆

A cigarette lighter
fished from the surf
still lit the candles
at our little feast.
Night drew in
about the house
and when we fell
into bed the sea
erased our names.

◆

The fever will not leave.
It will teach us waiting.
I write by the light of the trees,
by moss and salal,
the black flash of raven wings,
by the slow mist